# *Dirty Dancing*™

## HOW TO DO IT

by Mimi Kasbah

A DELL TRADE PAPERBACK

A DELL TRADE PAPERBACK
Published by
Dell Publishing
a division of
The Bantam Doubleday Dell Publishing Group, Inc.
666 Fifth Avenue
New York, New York 10103

ISBN: 0-440-50167-9

Printed in the United States of America
Published simultaneously in Canada

October 1988

10 9 8 7 6 5 4 3 2 1

SM

Grateful acknowledgment is made to the following:
Sylvain and Irene at Michaelis/Carpelis Design Associ-
ates, Marilyn Abraham of Dell Publishing, Al Reuben,
Susan Senk and Leslie Rotenberg of Vestron, Sharon
Squibb and Angela Miller of IMG.

The writer, Mimi Kasbah, thanks Willie Rosario,
Richard and Joni.

And, finally, a very special thanks to Eleanor
Bergstein, Emile Ardolino, Kenny Ortega, Baby
and Johnny.

Billboard 1963 year-end chart © 1988 by Billboard
Publications, Inc. Reprinted with permission.

The dance steps described herein were performed by
professionally trained dancers. Some of the steps
involve strenuous physical movements which should
not be attempted without *proper conditioning or*
professional guidance. None of the steps should be
attempted by anyone with health problems.

# HOW TO DO IT

# CONTENTS

# CHAPTER ONE

# What is Dirty Dancing?

"(I Had the) Time of My Life"

Dirty Dancing is a phenomenon. Dirty Dancing is communication. Dirty Dancing is the joy of movement, of dance, of feeling the beat and the heat.

Dirty Dancing is a state of mind.

"Dirty Dancing," said screenwriter Eleanor Bergstein, "is dancing your heart out."

For one thing, there's really nothing very dirty about it! Sensual and uninhibited, yes. It's style…it's steps…it's attitude.

As choreographer Kenny Ortega, best-known for his sensational steps for the sizzling movie *Salsa* as well as for Madonna's famous "Material Girl" video, explained, he based the dances in the movie on "all the original dancing of the early sixties. Dirty Dancing is like soul dancing, only with a partner. A little Mambo is thrown in, a little Cuban

motion…a conglomeration of rhythms and movements.

"And because it is soul dancing, it's something that comes out as an expression. It's not about technique as much as it is about feeling."

For Baby, Dirty Dancing became the way to discover herself and her body and her emerging sexuality as a woman. For Johnny it became the way to find his self-respect, to show how much he really loved his Baby.

"Dirty Dancing is the most erotic form of partner dancing," the film's director, Emile Ardolino, elaborated. And he should know. He won the Oscar in 1984 for his documentary *He Makes Me Feel Like Dancing*, and he has produced and/or directed twenty-eight programs in the acclaimed public television series "Dance in America," among

## SOME GREAT GIRL-GROUP SONGS FROM THE EARLY SIXTIES

| Group | Song Title |
|---|---|
| Ad-Libs | The Boy From New York City |
| Angels | My Boyfriend's Back |
| Chiffons | One Fine Day |
| Cookies | Chains; Don't Say Nothin' Bad |
| Crystals | Uptown; He's a Rebel; Then He Kissed Me |
| Skeeter Davis | End of the World |
| Dixie Cups | Chapel of Love |
| Lesley Gore | You Don't Own Me; It's My Party |
| Little Eva | The Locomotion |
| Darlene Love | Today I Met the Boy I'm Gonna Marry |
| Martha and the Vandellas | Dancing in the Streets; Heat Wave |
| Marvelettes | Please Mr. Postman; Beechwood 4-5789 |
| Orlons | Wah-Wahtusi; Don't Hang Up; South Street |
| Raindrops | What a Guy |
| Ronettes | Be My Baby; Walkin' in the Rain |
| Dee Dee Sharp | Mashed Potatoes |
| Shirelles | Will You Still Love Me Tomorrow; Baby It's You |
| Supremes | Where Did Our Love Go; Baby Love |

many others. *Dirty Dancing* writer Eleanor Bergstein called him "the only director in the world who can make you understand not only what dancing looks like, but what it feels like to *be* dancing!"

"A few years later," Ardolino went on, "when people started dancing away from each other, what was lost was the wonderful experience of taking someone in your arms and dancing cheek to cheek or hip to hip or shoulder to shoulder. Touching each other, communicating with each other, that's what dancing has always been. If two people are dancing, looking into each other's eyes and trying to convey 'I Love You,' that's the most intimate kind of communication, the most intimate outside the bedroom."

And it's not dirty at all!

During the fifties and sixties as well as now, Dirty Dancing was never just about "sex." If anything, it was about discovery, of getting loose, of pushing yourself only as far as you wanted to go.

"If *Dirty Dancing* does one thing," Jennifer Grey remarked, "I hope it will show kids what it feels like to be really connected to someone without jumping into bed. Dancing is a form of safe sex!"

"What we got away with on the dance floor was it," remembered Kenny Ortega. "That *was* the weekend!"

"My huge interest was in dancing," said Eleanor Bergstein. After all, *Dirty Dancing* was based on her own life and experiences. "And I think there were so many taboos in those years that most of our energy went into the dancing itself."

She added, "Back then, kids weren't really having sex. It wasn't like dancing now, which refers to what you were doing before and what you're going to do later. This took the place of it.

"I would practice steps in front of the full-length mirror, and then would go around at night to the Dirty Dance contests....It was a central passion, and when the contests were over, we would just kind of sit in the car and look at the bridge until we went home. We just lived to do those kinds of steps."

"It happened," said Ortega. "It wasn't called Dirty Dancing"–at least not where he grew up–"but Liberated Dancing or Dirty Dawging. A lot of us kids did it and got in trouble for it!"

"I don't call it Dirty Dancing," said Cynthia Rhodes, the marvelous dancer who played Penny in the movie, "but free dancing, as it's very expressive. It's very exciting, very sensual, very hot, and a lot of fun.

"We dance hip to hip and shoulder to shoulder and cheek to cheek in a real sensuous way. But it's the music that makes it happen."

And the music in *Dirty Dancing* did make it happen, in large part due to Eleanor Bergstein.

"I knew what music I wanted played behind every scene," she said. "There was a lot of pressure against the old songs, because people thought no one wanted them anymore–that kids weren't interested in them anymore. My position was very ferocious, which was that the film made no sense without them. They were as much a part of the film and story and idea and characters as Baby and Johnny."

Bergstein also had sixty pages of dance instructions to go with her screenplay.

"It was the first time," Kenny Ortega remarked, "I've ever read a script where every single time there was a dance mentioned, there was a specific piece of music and a specific direction that dance needed to move towards."

There were basically three styles of dancing in the movie:

1. Traditional ballroom (like the Foxtrot) and Latin dancing (Merengue, Mambo, Cha-cha);

2. Dirty Dancing–what the staff kids did in their quarters after work;

3. Johnny and Baby's last Mambo–the one performed to "(I Had the) Time of My Life"–which was a marriage of the Mambo and Dirty Dancing moves.

These were based on Eleanor Bergstein's own experiences growing up in Brooklyn and Dirty Dancing in the late fifties and early sixties. She really did take Mambo and Cha-cha lessons in

Ballroom dancing at its finest.

**Penny and Johnny Dirty Dancing.**

the Catskills on summer vacations; and she, like Johnny, became an Arthur Murray dance instructor, where she learned how to break a dance down into its elements and explain it to students. Her background and talent as a writer created the indelibly stamped images and dances in *Dirty Dancing*. Why, even the choreographer, Kenny Ortega, had to audition for her!

"Eleanor said to me, 'I think you're great and I love your energy and I like your ideas,' " Ortega explained, " 'but I won't be able to give you the gig till you Dirty Dance with me.' That was the scariest part of the whole thing!"

Emile Ardolino, who was also there, said, "I was very embarrassed. I thought maybe I shouldn't be looking!"

Eleanor Bergstein added: "Kenny and I said, 'No, you don't understand. It's not Dirty Dancing unless there's a third person present!' "

## THE CAST

Patrick Swayze was always the first choice for Johnny, because he could act and dance so well, but finding the perfect actress to play Baby was more difficult. Before any actress was permitted to read her lines, she had to audition for the dancing.

Baby and Johnny's Last Mambo.

## DIRTY DANCING: A CRITIC'S EYE VIEW

Since the film has become such a hit, critics have fallen all over themselves trying to describe just exactly what Dirty Dancing is. What could have been running through Baby's mind when Billy opened the door to the smoke-filled and steamy and completely unexpected world of Dirty Dancing? One critic said it succinctly when writing that Baby's eyes were opened to "dancing with an intimacy and insinuation that shocks and mesmerizes her."

Here are a few select morsels gleaned from reviews and stories that appeared across America and Europe:

- Outrageously sultry
- Ultimate makeout party
- Intimate writhing with which young people once heated family basements on the sly
- A swaying and pounding both stylized and personal
- Pulsating and infectious movements and sounds
- An erotic form of touch dancing
- A passionate expression of sexuality; dancing as a way of getting at sex and freedom
- Eye-opening writhing and wriggling, swaying and pounding that's half-sex, half-dance, and all sincerity
- A sultry form of moving while holding each other close
- Lowdown and sultry and disreputable
- A sensual, sexual grinding, up-close tribal ritual that's all their own
- Undreamed-of physicality
- The next best thing to sex

There is, after all, a world of difference between the sexual and the sensual—and that is precisely what Baby learns in her summer of Dirty Dancing.

Perhaps film critic Carrie Rickey summed it up best when she wrote: "*Dirty Dancing* does for touch dancing 1960s style what Astaire and Rogers did for ballroom swing-and-sway. That is, to illustrate how dancing expresses one's most intimate feelings."

"We wanted to see actresses who could move in some unique way before I read them," explained Ardolino. "Jennifer walked in and I knew immediately she was Baby. She came in with these adorable flesh-colored tights, bare midriff, and sneakers, with her hair all piled up on top. And she moved in a unique quirky way and she was childlike and sexy at the same time. I felt I could help her make a believable transition from this girl who's all scrunched up and doesn't think she's attractive to someone who gets a whole different attitude about her body and her being."

Jennifer Grey had taken many dance classes–in ballet, tap, Caribbean, and jazz–but certainly never considered herself a professional dancer. Besides, Ardolino didn't want a professional for Baby; he was not going to use a "dance double" (like the one used in *Flashdance*) and was prepared to adjust the choreography to the ability of the actress he cast.

"He needed someone who was a natural dancer," Jennifer explained, "who didn't necessarily have to have any training but who could move well." That she did, in grueling rehearsal sessions that continued well into the actual filming.

Rehearsal clothes for a Cha-cha.

"We rehearsed for a few weeks before the company ever showed up and then after we started shooting," Patrick Swayze said. "If I weren't working a day or in the morning we'd jump into a rehearsal–we'd sometimes shoot all day and rehearse till midnight, two o'clock in the morning and be back up early to shoot."

"We workshopped with eight principal dancers, and came up with what I think is a really wonderful idea based on an authentic dance style of the early sixties period," Ortega explained. "This is about my eleventh picture as a choreographer and it doesn't feel like anything I've ever done before. There's a lot more dancing in it for one thing, and the dancing has a lot more to do with the continuity of the story and the development of the characters, where in other musical pictures the dancing sometimes and often is separated from the story. This picture will really inspire people to get back out there and really dance together.

"I've never worked with a trained dance lead before," he went on, speaking of Swayze. "As a choreographer, it was very exciting to think I was actually going to be spending time with somebody who already had years of experience and that we weren't going to have to go through a basic training program to get this person to look good on the screen. In that respect it was wonderful to work with Patrick.

"He was so open to taking from me and I was so willing to give. Of course he has tremendous strengths in his technique we tried to work with to provide some strong support for him to use, and at the same time he was playing a Latin-born street kid. I wanted him to be a soulful character as a dancer. It wasn't hard."

Ironically, Patrick didn't think of *Dirty Dancing* as his "dance film." "Because," he explained, "Johnny Castle is from the streets of South Philadelphia, you know. So he's no virtuoso.

"My character isn't as good of a dancer as I am. He didn't have the training. Johnny learned from Arthur Murray. I studied jazz, ballet, modern, tap all my life, as well as having danced profes-

sionally with ballet companies in New York City.

"It was a struggle with the ego. But I got away with one moment, very technical, at the end, when I come off the stage, do a double turn in the air, then down on the knee. That's the one liberty I took but the ego has to be contained in order to stay true to a character."

"I need to blow it out somewhere. My first dance film and I've got to pull back? You want to stretch yourself."

As for Jennifer Grey learning how to move, as Kenny put it, "Although she doesn't have much experience as a dancer, she has dance in her background and she's a very quick learner, and a very, very dedicated woman. She worked hours and hours and hours to make something right. She's a perfectionist, and I love that. Always doing her best to make my work look better."

But for Kenny, Cynthia Rhodes is unequalled. "She is the ultimate professional in my eyes," he went on. "She is stylish beyond belief–those legs, that line, her enthusiasm. She has a back with no bones in it and legs that you have to put a stop sign on. She makes my work really come alive and look so much better than it would on just anyone."

"Kenny is really talented," said Jennifer Grey. "He knew how to make me look good and feel comfortable and how to use what I could do to all of our advantages.

"This was by far the most challenging thing I'd ever done...the stamina alone was a challenge. And then to dance–I'd *never* done anything like it before, ever– I've never danced in front of anyone except the kids in dance class. So when we shot the Mambo with 350 extras and 100 crew and the lights–it was very exciting, very exhilarating, and *very* scary!

"I did what I could," she added modestly. "I was just trying not to step on anybody's toes!"

What she didn't have to fake was her apprehension about the lift, but there was no way to use a double for that all-important scene at the end. "I *was* scared," Jennifer admitted. "After all, Patrick is six feet tall and I was high! But he said, 'I've never dropped anyone, ever.'" Obviously, he knew what he was doing, and was not about to let go of his Baby.

"Jennifer was amazing," Patrick said. "She's got an incredible natural talent. She jumped into this stuff and it's not easy dancing at all. And she just took it over and made it her own and has come out with a sensuality in her dancing which has just staggered everybody. There's a real power in our eyes when we dance together–it's fun, it's nice, and it makes it a lot more interesting for me when you're playing with that connection in the eyes and how hot you can make it."

## SHALL WE DANCE?

"They were a pair of American folk dancers, glorious ones to be sure, but all their glory flowed from the fact that we could sing their songs and at least imagine ourselves doing their dances," wrote the well-known dance critic Arlene Croce. "She's an American classic, just as he is: Common clay that we prize above exotic marble. The difference between them is that he knew and she didn't."

Was she writing about Patrick Swayze and Jennifer Grey and the music of *Dirty Dancing*? Sure sounds like it. But she was, instead, referring to the inimitable Fred Astaire and Ginger Rogers and the films they made more than forty years ago. They were sensual, they were fluidly graceful, they embodied all it meant to dance in perfect harmony with your partner. If *Dirty Dancing* has piqued anyone's interest in ballroom dancing and all its variations, then a quick trip to the video store or a movie revival house should be a number one priority.

The best of the Astaire/Rogers films are: *Top Hat*, *Follow the Fleet*, *Swing Time*, and *Shall We Dance*. And if you're interested in the dance crazes of the pre-World War II era, check out Fred and Ginger in *The Story of Vernon and Irene Castle*, based on the famous couple who were as innovative in their day as Dirty Dancers were then.

Fans of fabulous dancing in the movies—especially those who liked watching the muscular Patrick Swayze go solo—should also see just about anything in which Gene Kelly appeared. (Swayze's muscular agility is more akin to Kelly's acrobatic ease than it is to Astaire's debonair sophistication. But the parallel between Fred and Ginger and Johnny and Baby still holds.) Have a ball with *Anchors Aweigh*, *On the Town*, *The Pirate*, *Invitation to the Dance*, *An American in Paris*, and, of course, *Singing in the Rain*.

And they certainly made it hot.

Patrick also learned a tremendous amount from Eleanor Bergstein. "The woman can get down. She can go for it!" he said. "She's this classy, intellectual kind of woman, and...hot stuff going on."

Of course, the most important thing Patrick had to do for this character was "to bring out a rough sexuality, an intense Marlon Brando type of heat. The dancing," Swayze said, "really helps to bring out the passion–it's the best way of releasing emotion."

It became the best way for Baby and Johnny to learn about each other–their strengths and weaknesses, hopes and desires.

"It's a film with a lot of heart," Swayze also said. "It has a sensual heat but I don't think you need to show explicit sex to create great passion. That only alienates the audience.

"Yes, the dancing in the film is steamy. We worked hard to try to make it look sexy....It's got to be done from reality or it doesn't work."

It was just that kind of charged energy that put to rest the notion that dancing's not "masculine" or macho. And Patrick Swayze was certainly the man for the job.

"There's a strong prejudice that men shouldn't dance, that it's not a strong hero thing to do," director Ardolino said. Actually, Dirty Dancing is quite a man's dance–he leads; he initiates all the moves. "But this movie certainly disproves it. It's more in a line of what Gene Kelly and Fred Astaire did. Dancing doesn't have to be feminine. It's a very strong physical expression of an emotion or personality."

That is what Dirty Dancing is all about: a strong physical expression of an emotion or personality. It's not just the steps. It's not just counting to the beat. It's fun. It's sexy. It's *feeling*.

One of the reasons *Dirty Dancing* became so tremendously successful was that in many ways it was like a fairy tale: The Ugly Duckling, Baby, is kissed by the Frog Prince, Johnny, and becomes a beautiful princess. But as she awakened to her life as a woman, she showed him what his life could mean as well. All their most intimate thoughts and feelings were expressed through dance.

As Patrick Swayze told Barbara Walters on her television Special: "Everybody dreams that somebody would see into their lonely world, that would see past the exterior and see what they're really like and care about them as a person. I think that's the biggest thing this film communicates–a relationship not because of how somebody swings their rear, but what's inside."

"I hope," echoed Ardolino, "we get the idea through that it's a great idea to be close to someone you care about."

And as Cynthia Rhodes said, "Being in the arms of someone you truly love to dance with, melting in the arms of someone who's a terrific partner–as Patrick was–then suddenly the world seems all right."

Once you understand what Dirty Dancing means, you're ready to get out there and show it off.

Director Emile Ardolino: "It's a great idea to be close to someone you care about."

## THE MUSIC OF *DIRTY DANCING*

Dirty Dancing is an ode to the early sixties. During the summer of 1963, music was changing in a dramatic way–Elvis, Chuck Berry, Chubby Checker had started it, and the Beatles were stirring up a storm in England. Spicy Latin rhythms were also emerging from the American melting pot. The world itself was on the cusp of a new way of thinking; the New Society hadn't yet given birth to the age of Aquarius. What was shocking to the guests at Kellerman's that sleepy summer would soon rule the airwaves.

The songs in 1963 were meant to stir the body as well as the emotions. There were words to think about as well as throbbing rhythms to feel.

What is the tune accompanying the sensational slowmotion opening credits? "Be My Baby" by the Ronettes. (This is before we even know the name of the leading lady is Baby.)

What does Baby hear when she sees Dirty Dancing for the first time? "Do You Love Me" by the Contours, and then the soulfully stirring "Love Man" by Otis Redding.

And what does she hear when she walks, for the second time, through the room full of sensuously swaying Dirty Dancers in search of Johnny and Penny? "Stay" by Maurice Williams and the Zodiacs.

The titles alone of the other period songs are evocative of other scenes: "Some Kind of Wonderful," "These Arms of Mine," "Cry," "Will You Still Love Me Tomorrow," "You Don't Own Me," and "In the Still of the Night." To say nothing of "Love Is Strange."

*Dirty Dancing* fans can practice all their steps to these oldies-but-goodies easily enough since the soundtrack albums, *Dirty Dancing* and *More Dirty Dancing* have topped the charts for months. Or you can check out the

oldies section at your local record store.

"I tried to choose the harshest music I could find, the music that would be the most sexually shocking to a young woman who'd never heard it before," explained Eleanor Bergstein. These lyrics would be straight and emotional, the beat would be steady and rhythmical, the messages would be clear, and the voices singing them pure, harmonious and soulful. Everyone knew all the lyrics and these songs made it impossible *not* to sing along. And the songs meant so much because they *said* so much.

One aspect of *Dirty Dancing* that's especially wonderful for music fans is that it has created a renewed interest in some of the great songs of the early sixties to an entirely new generation. At the *Dirty Dancing* tour that started in late May of 1988, fans of all ages–from 8 to 88–filled the audiences around America, and sang along to all the songs. It was an exercise in nostalgia for parents and an exercise in delight (and dancing in their seats) for youngsters who particularly loved Merry Clayton's ''Yes,'' Eric Carmen's ''Hungry Eyes,'' and, of course, Bill Medley singing ''(I've Had the) Time of My Life.''

The tour was living proof that *Dirty Dancing*'s appeal had become universal.

Latin fans will also want to hurry to record stores to find great dance music to Mambo and Merengue by. Of course, ''(I Had the) Time of My Life'' will always remain a wonderful song to Mambo to.

## BILLBOARD TOP RHYTHM & BLUES SINGLES OF SUMMER 1963

Pos.   TITLE–Artist (Label)

1. PART TIME LOVE–*Little Johnny Taylor* (Galaxy)
2. MOCKINGBIRD–*Inez Foxx* (Symbol)
3. BABY WORKOUT–*Jackie Wilson* (Brunswick)
4. FINGERTIPS (Part II)–*Little Stevie Wonder* (Tamla)
5. HEAT WAVE–*Martha & the Vandellas* (Gordy)
6. PRIDE AND JOY–*Marvin Gaye* (Tamla)
7. THE LOVE OF MY MAN–*Theola Gilgore* (Serock)
8. CRY BABY–*Garnett Mimms & the Enchanters* (United Artists)
9. YOU'VE REALLY GOT A HOLD ON ME–*Miracles* (Tamla)

Pos.   TITLE–Artist (Label)

10. HELLO STRANGER–*Barbara Lewis* (Atlantic)
11. JUST ONE LOOK–*Doris Troy* (Atlantic)
12. THE MONKEY TIME–*Major Lance* (Okeh)
13. THAT'S THE WAY LOVE IS–*Bobby Bland* (Duke)
14. OUR DAY WILL COME–*Ruby & the Romantics* (Kapp)
15. HE'S SO FINE–*Chiffons* (Laurie)
16. IF YOU WANNA BE HAPPY–*Jimmy Soul* (S.P.Q.R.)
17. TWO LOVERS–*Mary Wells* (Motown)
18. EASIER SAID THAN DONE–*Essex* (Roulette)
19. MICKEY'S MONKEY–*Miracles* (Tamla)
20. WALK LIKE A MAN–*Four Seasons* (Vee Jay)

How's this for a Dirty Dance partner?

# CHAPTER TWO

# THE DANCES IN DIRTY DANCING

Penny leads the guests in a Merengue class.

### MERENGUE LESSON

"God wouldn't have given you maracas if he didn't want you to shake 'em!" Penny shouts enthusiastically to her class of oldsters–and youngsters, like a hapless Baby–with two left feet. Undaunted, Penny uses her inimitable sense of humor to keep the room lively–and it isn't difficult once the lively 4/4 beat begins.

As the men and women form circles and move in opposite directions–a round-robin, partner-choosing step reminiscent of the famous gym scene in *West Side Story*–Penny calls out: "When I say stop, you're gonna find the man of your dreams!" That wasn't quite true for Baby, who found herself partnered with a sweet little old lady, quite possibly the only female at Kellerman's who's shorter than she is. Not exactly what she'd hoped for in a dance partner!

"1–2–3–4, stomp those feet and stomp some more!" Penny calls out as the dancers move from side-to-side. "Now remember–he's the boss on the dance floor if nowhere else!"

## MAMBO!!

"Mambo! Yeah! Come on!" Even Neil, the stiff "catch of the county," or so he like to call himself, gets excited when he hears the musical introduction to the Mambo. Yet Neil doesn't "teach" Baby the Mambo–he just "leads" her in the moves. Baby is still stiff and unsure of herself, and she'd rather look at the other couples to see what they're doing. And when Johnny and Penny begin their routine, she couldn't have hoped for a better couple to watch. "They shouldn't be showing off with each other," Neil complains (wrongly!). "That's not going to sell dance lessons."

Watch the feet of the other couples during this scene–it's a good way to see people dancing the basic steps of the Mambo. Only experienced dancers can do the spins, lifts, and intricate steps that Johnny and Penny performed.

Baby does not look pleased with her father's comments to Neil, the self-proclaimed "catch of the county."

You need professional dance training to attempt moves like these—but they certainly are sensational.

## Introduction to Dirty Dancing

"Can you keep a secret?" Johnny's cousin Billy asks Baby. "Your parents would kill you. Max would kill me!" And then he pushes open the doors and Baby's life will change forever.

She's never seen anything like Dirty Dancing.

"Wanna try it?" Billy asks her.

She shakes her head no, vehemently. (Never has her name seemed so appropriate!)

As she winds her way through a sea of sweaty, sexy, undulating bodies, Baby's completely shocked. No, she can't imagine seeing any of this on the main dance floor, home of the family Fox-trot.

Do you remember the wonderful scene in the movie when Baby, who has discovered Dirty Dancing for the first time, gets her first lesson from a steamy Johnny Castle?

When "Love Man" comes on, Johnny can't resist the urge to break the Kellerman's taboo and teach the guest's daughter a few tricks. He beckons to her with his index finger, and for a few panicked seconds she looks around helplessly, as if she can't believe he's really chosen her. With a last glance at her friend Billy, she allows herself to be drawn into the crowd.

Johnny places his hands on Baby's shoulders and tells her to bend her knees. Her rear end sticks out and she's stiff with anxiety and embarrassment. Poor Baby! She looks like a duck out of water. As Johnny starts rotating his pelvis, Baby tries a pale imitation, and

Baby's first lesson in Dirty Dancing.

## HOW TO THROW A DIRTY DANCE PARTY

Roll up the carpet.

Turn up the air conditioning.

Stock the refrigerator with lots of water and juice.

Crank up the music. (*Dirty Dancing* and *More Dirty Dancing* soundtrack albums will do fine, thank you.)

Invite equal numbers of men and women.

Get down and dirty!

A few more tips:

Make sure anything breakable is out of the way.

Try to have a few more experienced dancers around who won't mind showing some new moves to the less experienced.

Show the video of *Dirty Dancing* for inspiration.

Have contests for most authentic costume. Try to have everyone come dressed in *Dirty Dancing* style.

Switch partners often to experience learning how to move with a new person.

Wear loose-fitting clothing so you don't get broiled alive.

Have a great time!

**If you plan to be very noisy, invite your neighbors and even your parents to join in the fun. Chances are they can teach *you* a few new moves!

then looks around to see what other people are doing.

No, Johnny tells her. "Watch my eyes. Good! That's better. Now roll this way." He grabs her waist, and they move from side to side. Next he puts her hands around his neck and leads her into a bumping, dipping, grinding dance, moving in perfect unison to the beat, their bodies as one.

And then, just as quickly as he taught her to move, he loosens his grip and walks–or rather saunters–away into the crowd. Baby, lost to the beat, twirls around and dances with herself for a moment. For the first time in her life she has felt the music. Then she catches herself, stops clapping, a bit embarrassed and surprised by how quickly she'd loosened up.

As quickly as Johnny came into her life, he was gone.

And after her first taste of Dirty Dancing, Baby is hungry for more. A lot more.

## MAMBO MAGIC LESSONS

Johnny tells her that you don't start till the two. Has she got it? Hardly. Baby's never danced any of these dances before. Relax, he tells her. Oh sure, that's a good one. Breathe, he says. Frame! Remember to stand straight. But

Dancing is like a heartbeat...a feeling...and with that Johnny teaches Baby how to move to the beat.

it's hard to stand straight when your stomach's all tied up in knots.

Here's what Johnny said to Baby when their dance lesson started:

2–3–4.

Don't lean back

Lifting up. (He holds her waist and back in the correct position.) Shoulders down.

Again.

2–3–4.

Now concentrate!

Don't put your heel down. (Your weight should be on the ball of your foot.)

Poor Baby. She practices her 2–3–4s on the steps of Kellerman's.

"The steps aren't enough," Johnny tells her. "Feel the music. It's a feeling, a heartbeat."

He places her hand on his chest and beats out his heart's rhythm with his hand atop hers–and very slowly starts to move...2...3...4...in time to the music.

Was there ever a more romantic way to learn to dance?

At their next lesson, Baby is getting better, but Johnny is still impatient with her, although he no longer has to count out 2–3–4.

"Head up," he says. "Frame. Lock it!"

Exasperated, he points to her arms.

"It's a feeling...a heartbeat."

Johnny clearly shows Baby the meaning of "dance space" and position as Penny looks on.

Baby is finally starting to get the hang of it.

"Look, spaghetti arms," he says. "This is my dance space." He indicated the circle of air before his arms. And then he indicates her dance space.

Penny comes over to join them. She places Baby's left arm on Johnny's right arm, and her left hand near his shoulder.

She places Baby's right palm down in Johnny's left hand.

Shoulders back.

Head up.

Then she puts her right hand on Baby's hips and left palm in the center of Baby's back.

They start to move, the three of them.

Baby nearly smiles. She's starting to get the hang of it.

There is a lovely scene in which Baby and Penny dance palm-to-palm. (The reason for this is to learn how to follow the subtle pressure from the man leading you, and also to learn the hip motion so integral to Latin dancing.)

In another endearing scene, Johnny teaches Baby the introduction to their Mambo number. He puts her arm up on his shoulder, drapes it around his neck, and he then runs his arm down her side in a slow, sensuous gesture.

She breaks out giggling. She's terribly ticklish!

After mastering most of the moves of the dance, it's time to learn lifts. Johnny teaches Baby about balance–the most important thing in lifts–while standing on a log above a trickling, rock-strewn creek. He leaps onto it and nearly falls off…and then cajoles Baby into dancing with him on the log.

**A study in balance.**

"You will hurt me if you don't trust me," Johnny tells Baby during the lift-practice session in a grassy field. She runs, bends her knees, springs up to his arms–and he lifts her.

But the best place to practice lifts is in the water, and so there they go. "Hold your position!" Johnny yells. But of course they fall over, screaming with laughter. Could it be they're falling in love?

As Baby gets dressed for their big Mambo number, she recites a litany of all the things she needs to remember for the dance. What if she forgets the steps?

Shoulders down.

Head up.

Frame locked.

Stay on your toes.

Tension in the arms.

Don't look at your feet.

Let him lead you!

Naturally, they make it through the Mambo Magic number, although Baby is too scared to do the lift. Never was anyone so happy to get through a dance!

## BABY AND JOHNNY'S PRIVATE DIRTY DANCING

''Dance with me,'' she says simply. And this time she doesn't have to be shown where to put her arms.

Johnny dips, bending her back, then swinging her in a circle. He pulls her leg up on his leg. She walks around him slowly. They hold each other close. This is a dance of possession, of womanhood, of surrender, of love.

A very private dance.

## CHA-CHA

Actually, the first time we saw the Cha-cha, the Housemans had come to the outdoor pavilion for the after-dinner dance, and Johnny was dancing with Vivian Pressman, one of the "bungalow bunnies" who'd been taking dance lessons from him. Vivian dances around Johnny and then in front of him, one of the characteristic moves of the Cha-cha, while running her fingers suggestively up and down his body (not one of the characteristic moves!).

Yet the Cha-cha Baby and Johnny attempt to do is more fun—and a lot looser. This time he can't keep his fingers from running suggestively all over Baby's body, and she lovingly mocks all his previous dance instructions to her as she tries to Cha-cha.

"My frame!" she says sarcastically. "Hey! Where's my pleasing arc? Spaghetti arms! Would you give me some tension, please! You're invading my dance space."

(This doesn't stop him from grabbing her.)

Let's Cha-cha.

"Love Is Strange."

### THE LAST DANCE

It starts out as the Mambo Magic number–to the strains of ''(I Had the) Time of My Life''–but with a difference...and what a difference those Dirty Dance moves make! In it, Johnny incorporated what he called ''a cross between Cuban rhythm and soul dancing.''

Turns and spins in Baby and Johnny's last dance.

Johnny leads the Dirty Dancers in the last glorious dance.

At one point, Johnny leaps off the stage and all the staff kids join him. Soon everybody discovers the fun of Dirty Dancing–did you catch Neil and Mrs. Houseman boogieing together? And everyone else joins in as well, copying the moves Baby and Johnny have showed them.

It was probably the sexiest Mambo ever choreographed.

Now, are you ready to Dirty Dance yourself?

Penny teaches a few Dirty dance moves to Dr. Houseman.

Even Mrs. Houseman can Dirty Dance with Neil.

The lift...it was not just about dancing—it was about trust.

# CHAPTER THREE

# How TO DIRTY DANCE: STEP-BY-STEP

Look at their alignment and footwork.

## DIRTY DANCE TIPS

A lot of people get stuck on the steps. The steps are *not* important! *The most important thing is STYLE!* Even if you can only do the simplest of steps and turns, you can still look like a million dollars.

It's all the way you hold your head, the way you look–your *attitude*.

Dirty Dancing *is* attitude. How you feel, how you project.

Dancing is easier if you try to form a different picture in your head for each dance you do–remember that every dance is different. For a Fox-trot think of a beautiful ballroom…for a Merengue you're on a beautiful beach, with palm trees swaying…for a Mambo you're in a steamy nightclub with a sexy gown and a sexier partner…and for Dirty

Dancing you're with someone who, well, who looks just like Patrick Swayze or Jennifer Grey.

When you form this picture in your mind, then you immediately find your proper attitude for dancing.

The biggest mistake people make is thinking they know how a dance *should* look. Just walk to the music and *forget* about dancing so you're open to learning new concepts properly.

And it does not matter if you screw up. Nobody's going to notice. Even if you fall on the floor–professionals do all the time!–just get up, that's it. It will only be a problem if you make a big thing about it. The show must go on!

You can never get too good. Even the best dancers go back to beginner's classes and they repeat the four elements of dance and the basic steps over and over again. That's how they stay good.

Now, turn on the music…

**Perfect posture. Perfect style.**

## GET READY TO DANCE

Anyone can learn how to dance–just think of it as walking to music. Don't worry about how you look. Dancing is whatever you want to do.

### *DIRTY DANCING*'s CREATOR, ELEANOR BERGSTEIN, EXPLAINS WHAT DIRTY DANCING IS

"The story of *Dirty Dancing* was rhythmed to the music of the early sixties when the beat and lyrical content of the songs were what was happening, when couples singing along to each other in cars or on dance floors were lip synching to their dreams. The lyrics were emotional, the beat sexual, insistent, and the dancing it led to was free and from the heart. This dancing–the lyrics as much as to the beat, a swaying and pounding both stylized and per-sonal–was the style called Dirty Dancing."

## DANCE POSITION FOR LATIN AND BALLROOM DANCING
### (Fox-trot, Merengue, Mambo, Cha-cha)

Partners face each other.

Feet together.

Woman lifts her arms, bends her elbows, and rests the left forearm–no spaghetti arms, please!–on the man's upper right arm. Right hand holds his left hand, with subtle pressure against the ball of his hand.

DANCE SPACE

Johnny: "This is my dance space!"

Your "Dance Space" is actually your resistance, the tension between the man and the women's upper bodies that tells you where you're going to go. Remember, the man leads and the woman follows. What you learn to do is to hold your ground, as if there's a mirror or glass in front of you–and you're going to lean a little bit to the mirror. If you let your elbows go, you'll crash!

You always want to maintain a certain tension in your arms.

The man exerts a very subtle pressure on the woman, and since she is usually

moving backward, it's easier for her this way. If this pressure isn't there she won't know which way to go!

A GOOD RESISTANCE EXERCISE

Man and woman, palm-to-palm–walk around the room, shifting direction only by exerting pressure on the palm.

### A FEW TIPS FOR GUYS–YOU DO ALL THE LEADING

Leading is hard work in touch dancing because you have to figure out what you're going to do next and always think ahead of time. You also have to make sure you don't crash into other couples.

Leading is not like "I'm a caveman– I lead you!" Simply, a man subtly indicates to a woman where he wants to go, and while he does so he keeps her in balance. The woman has to trust him or else she'll tense up and lose her step and look awful! So treat her nicely!

A good exercise for leading is for the woman to switch places with the man– that teaches her resistance and how to think ahead. It also improves her own style and posture (and makes her appreciate just how hard it can be to lead).

Baby learns to Cha-cha. Actually, Baby gives Johnny a lesson in "dance space." Note that hip motion.

### LISTEN FOR THE BEAT

Everyone can, if they want to, learn how to count to the beat. You just have to teach yourself to listen for the back beat–the spine of the song. This is almost always supplied by the drums and bass (the deepest guitar sound). Put on any dance song you like. First tap along to the drum–the bom-bom-bom sound. You'll find yourself instinctively tapping 1–2–3–4.

Now, see where you place the emphasis–the accent. It can fall on the first, second, third, or fourth beat. It's wherever you hear it. In the Mambo Johnny taught Baby, he heard it on the second, and that's where they started.

Try tapping along with lots of different songs. Until you can unerringly keep the beat to any piece of music, keep practicing.

Another good exercise is to listen to a

Johnny leads Penny and she knows exactly where to go (even though they're side by side and not looking at each other)!

song and isolate all the instruments:
drums
percussion (cymbals, maracas, tambourines, etc.)
bass
guitar
keyboards (like the piano or synthesizer)
strings
horns

Follow the beat of each specific instrument all the way through.

**THE FOUR ELEMENTS OF DANCE**
Start each of these moves separately. Putting them together creates a dance. Practice them as much as you need to.

1. FORWARD AND BACK WALK
    1. Walk forward a few steps, relax.
    2. Now walk backward.

Rocking Step—shifting weight back and forth.

2. SIDE TOGETHER
   1. Step to the side with the Right Foot.
   2. Close with the Left Foot.
   3. Repeat to the left.

3. ROCKING STEP

This is what Baby practiced on Kellerman's steps to the sounds of ''Wipeout.'' It is absolutely essential to master this to do the Mambo correctly.

   1. Feet together.
   2. Step back with the Right Foot, heel up. Keep your weight on ball of the Right Foot.
   3. Shift weight to Left Foot, rocking yourself forward.
   4. Bring feet together.
   5. Repeat: Left Foot forward.           1
           Step in place with Right Foot. 2
           Feet together.                  3

To do this correctly you must step back OR forward without actually moving or traveling. By the time you have repeated the step with your right foot and then the left, you should be back in exactly the same place you started from. You simply shift your weight to get the rocking action.

**STRIPPING DOWN**

The most important Dirty Dancing requirement is comfort. If it feels good and you can move in it, great. Probably the worst thing you can wear is an ultra-tight pair of jeans, especially if you're planning to dance for hours and hours (jeans can become very uncomfortable and constricting if you sweat a lot).

It's fun for Dirty Dancers to take a few sartorial tips from Baby, Johnny, Penny, and the other Dirty Dancers in the movie. Did you notice that, as Baby became more confident and relaxed with her body during her dance lessons with Johnny, her clothing became more comfortable and revealing as well? Gone were the prissy little belted cotton dresses and overstretched mohair sweaters she wore when dancing with the insufferably smug Neil, grandson of Max Kellerman. They were replaced by loose white jeans and a blue plaid button-down shirt (still pretty stiff) and white sneakers. (Such things as

jogging shoes or aerobics hadn't been invented yet.) Then, as the lesson progresses, her shirt gets rolled up and tied at her midriff. And by the time she is practicing the Mambo's steps up and down the Kellerman's steps–to the wacky beat of "Wipeout"–she is clad only in a flesh-colored, body-hugging leotard and cut-off shorts. (She wears cut-offs again, with a rolled-up button-down shirt, during her hilariously sensual lip sync with Johnny to Mickey and Sylvia's "Love Is Strange." It was an unusual way to learn to Cha-cha!)

This scene shifts to a palm-to-palm practice session with Penny, as Johnny looks on, tapping out the beat, and by now Baby is beginnning to look like a dancer. She has on only a cropped white top and dance tights rolled down at the hips, leaving much of her torso bare. (This makes it much easier to see the proper alignment of the body and to maintain posture while turning.) And her feet have made a remarkable Cinderella-like transformation from rubber-soled white sneakers (how'd they stay so clean?!) to delicately strapped and silvery dance shoes.

The very last indoor lesson finds Baby looking even more like a pro—in a bra top and flowing chiffon skirt and proper dance shoes.

For her first professional dance appearance during the Mambo Magic number, Baby wears a glamorous red chiffon dress (fit to her by Penny in an endearing scene, though she modestly kept her plain white cotton bra on) that swirls and twirls and accentuates every turn. It's the kind of dress dancers wear to make a dramatic impression. And her white dress for the last dance has a fitted bodice with a scoop neck and flowing skirt. Not as flashy, of course, but perfect for her chraracter.

The pink dress Penny wears while dancing the Mambo with Johnny at Kellerman's shows off her stunning figure remarkably. With a tight, lace bodice—backless except for crisscross lacing—and yards of chiffon skirt, it allowed her full freedom in back bends and splits. This dress was a more daring and dressy version of the red dress she'd been wearing while teaching Baby's first Merengue class. (Did you notice how she kept one corner of the skirt in her hand and provocatively swished it back and forth in time to the music?)

When she rehearses Baby with Johnny, Penny wears only a black or red leotard, cinched by a belt, and fishnet tights. Slightly older viewers of *Dirty Dancing* may well have remembered that the filmmakers took a little artistic license with the legwear. After all, pantyhose had not quite been invented in 1963! (Dancers wore flesh-colored tights or fishnets for practice.) Luckily, women now have lots more options when it comes to covering or uncovering their legs.

Of course, just about any garment looked great on Johnny Castle. In fact, most women who've seen *Dirty Dancing* upteen times would agree that Johnny Castle looks best with as little on as possible.

When Johnny dances the Mambo with Penny, he is wearing—what else?—a black tuxedo, although this one is slightly more spiffy than usual with a cropped toreador jacket. He wore the same toreador tux, with a high cumberbund, white shirt with a wing collar, and loose tie for his performance with Baby. He'd also been seen dancing with a white dinner jacket one night with the guests.

But for the Dirty Dancing with the staff kids after-hours, Johnny flung off the tux jacket he'd been wearing, tore off his bow tie, unbuttoned as many buttons of his stiff white shirt as he could, and let it rip. Proof that you can Dirty Dance in just about anything.

When Johnny rehearses Baby, he progresses from a blue cotton shirt, to

Practicing underarm turns and breaks.

a more-unbuttoned blue cotton shirt, to tee shirts, to no shirts at all. But he always wears snug–not tight–black trousers and sturdy black leather ("Cuban") dancing shoes with one to one-and-a-half-inch heels. (These helped to keep his weight shifted to the ball of his foot, which is essential for proper dance technique.)

Perhaps Johnny's most memorable outfit was what he wore when lip synching with Baby to "Love Is Strange." In contrast to her white top and denim cut-offs, he is wearing the skimpiest of black undershirts and his trademark black trousers and shoes. The better to see those pecs, my dear!

For the last dance, led traditionally by Johnny (but this year it's certainly not going to be the traditional Mambo) Johnny has on a simple, short-sleeved, cropped, navy button-down shirt and trousers. Extremely casual gear, but Johnny still managed to make it look as sparingly elegant and sensual as possible.

4. FEET TOGETHER
  1. Feet together.
  2. Move a step to the right with the Right Foot.
  3. Close up with Left Foot.
  4. Move a step to the right again with the Right Foot.
  5. Close up again with the Left Foot. End up with your weight resting on the ball of your Left Foot–like you were tap dancing.
  6. Repeat to the left. The rhythm is 1–2–3–tap.

This is what Baby did when she was trying to learn the Merengue.

Next, we'll give you the basic steps to a few dances, and soon you'll be able to add whatever turns and spins and breaks you like into your routines–make them up as you go along. That's half the fun!

UNDERARM TURN
Every time you think of turning, think about keeping your right foot in place. Do not step or move with it. (That is called traveling.) Instead, pivot around with your left foot, using your right foot as an axis. Only your right heel comes up. The man gently turns you under his arm.

You simply twirl around in place, to a count of 1–2–3–4.

Underarm turn...into a spin.

**CROSS-BODY LEAD**

This step is used to take a couple from one side of the room to another. Remember when Johnny whispered it to Baby when they were doing their Mambo at the Sheldrake?

1. Backward Rocking Step.
2. Move forward. Woman crosses in front of man.
3. Weight is on Left Foot.

Cross-body Lead—traveling around the room.

## OPEN BOX STEP

This is also used for traveling around the room. You will be tracing a box with your feet. Basically you move back–side–forward and forward–side–back. The rhythm is quick-quick-step.

1. Step back with Right Foot.
2. Move to side with Left Foot.
3. Step over and across with Right Foot.

4. Move forward with Left Foot.
5. Go to side with Right Foot.
6. Close up to starting position.

You can also do this with a hop as Johnny and Baby did: 1–2–3–hop, back-side-forward-hop, and forward-side-back-hop.

Open Box Step—also used for traveling around the room.

## DIRTY DANCING CLOTHES

The Dirty Dancers in the movie wore an eclectic mix of clothing–anything from madras shorts and short-sleeved polka-dot shirts to halter-top dresses with short twirly skirts. In the last dance, for example, Penny wears a red off-the-shoulder top with puffy sleeves and fat black polka dots, along with very slim black pants. Other dancers simply threw on some pedal-pushers and tee shirts–very casual stuff, but they all managed to look sensationally sexy.

If you really want to look authentic, local antique or used clothing stores can outfit you in real styles from the early sixties. A raid in your parents, friends, or neighbors' closets may also be useful. Or try attics, local rummage sales–any used clothing outlet.

Again, what's most important is to feel comfortable (and sexy). Many women who are beginning dancers feel much better in a flippy skirt–even if you miss a beat during a turn, your skirt will still whoosh around and make you look great. If you're taking dance lessons, it's also absolutely essential for your dance teacher to be able to see your knees and make sure you're doing the movements properly.

If you plan to study Latin dances, you will find it much easier if you wear proper dance shoes with one- to two-inch heels. Since your weight must shift forward to the ball of your foot, it's essential to have the right shoes or it's much more difficult to do the steps correctly. Local dancewear shops should have them in stock, and they are usually not expensive at all.

So the basic rule for Dirty Dancing dressing is that just about anything goes. Study the dancers in the film. Wear anything you like that feels good and is not too close-fitting, unless it is modern dancewear like leotards. Skirts for girls can be a lot of fun, especially when worn over yards of petticoats–you can find them in many department stores or antique boutiques. Guys can don just about anything, too. Just be sure you like what you're wearing–an extra dose of confidence is always a boost when you're learning anything new.

## BASIC HIP MOTION

Ever wonder why some dancers look fabulous and others don't? It's all in the hips–and either you've got it–or you MUST learn how to get it!

Basically, while you're doing the Rocking Step, you move your hips from side to side by shifting your weight from knee to knee. This automatically moves the hips. This motion is difficult because your feet are also moving at the same time. The only way to get your proper hip motion is to be like Baby and practice, practice, practice. When "Wipe-out" started, she stamped her feet in frustration–but after working on this movement she had it down like a pro. Put on some beat-heavy music and move to it in front of a full-length mirror. It will take some sweat, but once you master the motion it's like learning to ride a bicycle. You'll never lose it.

Baby practices her Mambo steps and hip motion on the steps leading up to the staff quarters at Kellerman's.

Hips in motion.

## WHAT YOU CAN LEARN IN A
## DIRTY DANCING CLASS

Kim Cappelin and Marcus Davis teach a Dirty Dancing course in Chicago, and Kim has a few tips based on their experiences:

The popularity of Dirty Dancing really threw me for a loop! It truly is a phenomenon. It's a dance style that is very sexual. And besides, people want a change–there are always changes in dance (like after *Saturday Night Fever, Flashdance,* and *Footloose,* to say nothing of break dancing).

Our course is basically for people to have fun. It's four sessions of one and one-half hours each, and after six hours the kids are really pretty good.

The dancing is very popular with women. They bring the men in who are a little reluctant at first, but by the fourth week both the men and women are amazingly improved.

What we teach in the class is:
• Knowing how to count
• What a beat is and how to find it– the more you dance on a beat, the better you look
• Body isolation exercises
• Hip movement and circles
• Upper body circles
• Making people comfortable. Believe me, there are times when *I* can't count–that's why I have a partner!
• How to move fluidly to look sexy
• The Grind (or Hip Circle). We teach it in 4/4 time. It's a circular hip movement, and rubbing up and down against each other.
• Updated versions of the line dances you see in the movies. (You saw a line dance in the first *Dirty Dancing* sequence–Penny and Johnny lead it just before he comes over to pull Baby onto the dance floor.)

By the time the course is over, just about everyone can do the steps in clubs and look like the kids in the movie–without the deep back bends or the lifts. You must have proper dance training to even try them! The only problem is that people think they'll look like Patrick Swayze when they leave–and with his body you're talking years of extensive training.

Of course, you can only go so far with steps. I can teach the basic movements, but style comes from each individual. We have to teach our students to add style…the way to look sexy.

And if you don't practice, you don't look good!

Baby shifts her weight by bending her knees—doing the steps with her hip motion.

1. Do a Rocking Step.
2. Put your weight on the Right Foot.
3. Flex your knee forward.
4. Keep feet in place.
5. Straighten your knee.
6. Shift weight to Left Foot and repeat.

Now don't give up–you'll get it sooner or later! Just think of how you're whittling away your waist and hips while you practice.

The hip motion is the laziest and easiest in the Merengue. You're body is actually swaying from side to side, and your hips move naturally with the steps. Practice it by doing the Merengue steps and walking backward and forward with them around the room.

Keep your hands on your waist–always at waist level when practicing the Hip Motion–for the proper balance.

## TOP LINE or "FRAME"

Try to keep your body rigid, but not stiff, from the waist up. That way you will have more control over your hips and legs, which is where you're moving most anyway. The top line is the hardest to control evenly because you're usually thinking about how the rest of you is moving.

Always stand straight. The space between your lower ribs and your hips must remain straight. Think good posture!

As Johnny said: "Keep your head up!"

Always look into your partner's eyes. Never look at your feet nor at anyone but your partner. This will help you keep your frame in position.

## BREAKS

A break is any change in movement— any forward, backward, sideways, or any movement in a direction other than the one you were headed in constitutes a break.

**Keep that frame in line!**

Four different breaks.

**OPEN BREAK**
Instead of doing the steps facing your partner, make a half-turn to the right.

1. Step back with Right Foot.
2. Shift your weight and body away from your partner, to the right.
3. Rocking Step with Left Foot.
4. Close up. Feet together.

## FOX-TROT

Kellerman's was jokingly referred to as the "home of the 'Family Fox-trot.'" Although the Fox-trot may be old-fashioned, it is a beautiful dance and easy to do. It's great for loosening up and listening to the beat.

The Fox-trot uses Dance Elements 1 and 2. The motion does not come from the hips but from the ankles and knees. Each move is done on a beat:

### Man
1. Move Left Foot forward.
2. Move Right Foot forward.
3. Slide Left Foot to side, after briefly joining Right Foot.
4. Right and Left Feet close.

### Woman
1. Move Right Foot backward.
2. Then move Left Foot backward.
3. Slide Right Foot to the side, after briefly joining Left Foot.
4. Left and Right Feet close.

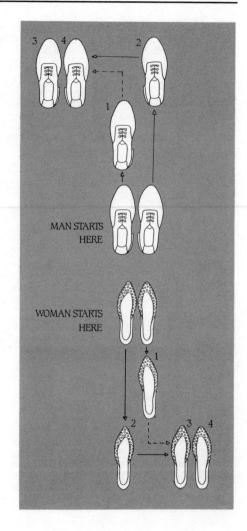

MAN STARTS HERE

WOMAN STARTS HERE

You should be gliding and turning around the room. The woman moves backward and the man moves forward, leading her.

"Kellerman's own" Tito Suarez (the great tap dancer Honi Coles) shows Max Kellerman a few moves.

## MERENGUE

The Merengue is a Latin dance using Element 4–Feet Together–and the Basic Hip Motion. The rhythm is step-step-step-tap. You will be moving side to side for a count of 4, for each side. Make each move on a beat.

*Man*

1. Move Left Foot to side, initiating movement with Right Hip.
2. Right and Left Feet close together.
3. Move Left Foot to side again, using stronger Right Hip power.
4. Right and Left close again. Repeat pattern.

*Woman:*

1. Follow your partner as a mirror image, using your hips to accentuate the movement.

You should end up in exactly the same position you started from–try to take steps that are all the same size. Once you have the steps, try adding a little hip motion to them.

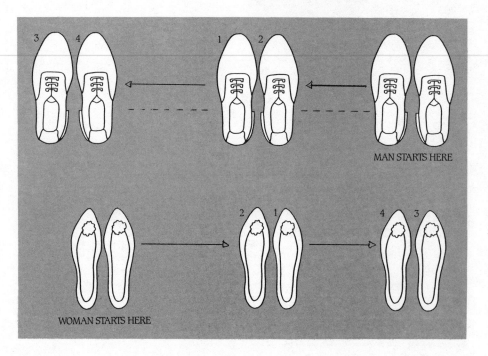

MAN STARTS HERE

WOMAN STARTS HERE

## YOUR DIRTY DANCING PARTNER

Believe it or not, one of the most difficult aspects of Dirty Dancing will be finding the perfect partner with whom to dance. You don't need a professional–much of the fun is learning together. But what you certainly do need is someone with the same commitment to learning, to repeating the same steps over and over again, and dedication to dancing that you have.

Here's what to look for in a partner.

### A Decent Sense of Rhythm

Musicality is crucial, because you move to music. Anyone can learn to hear the beat, but it takes time. If you're frustrated with your partner's tin ear–some people, unfortunately, simply do not have a strong sense of rhythm–it may be better to find someone else than risk losing a friend!

### Patience

Learning any new skill takes discipline and a willingness to make mistakes in the process. Remember Baby stomping her feet and screaming in frustration on the bridge as she started to practice the Mambo? She persevered despite all her doubts–and really learned to shake it. You and your partner can do just about anything if you stick with it.

### Height/Body Type

Most dancers do not look like Johnny, Penny, or Baby. Height or weight really do not matter, as long as you feel comfortable with your partner. Many people only feel relaxed if the man is taller than the woman, but accomplished dancers can swing, twirl, and lift just about anyone.

"We have a man who's six feet seven inches and he dances with a woman who's five feet two inches in

our class," one Dirty Dance instructor said. "Her head just about comes up to his waist–but they love to dance and actually look great together."

It's more important to like your partner than to worry about height–and a fabulous short dancer can still make you feel ten feet tall. (Forget their extra poundage, too. Dancing is a great way to tone up and slim down. Wanting to look sleek on the dance floor is a terrific incentive for would-be dieters.)

A Great Sense of Humor
Like Baby, you're going to step all over your partner's feet at first. Everybody–even the most accomplished pros–accepts the fact that you can easily slip, trip, and unexpectedly wind up on your derriere. It's hardly worth getting upset if you blow it once in a while, so a sympathetic and fun partner is a must. You need to laugh at your mistakes, not dwell on them. Being relaxed is absolutely essential. If you're rigid, it will be difficult to do any steps or turns properly.

Listen to the music. Close your eyes. Feel the beat. Relax…and move together to it.

Before long, what you thought was so difficult will seem as natural as breathing.

Here's what Patrick Swayze had to say about partnering:

"The fun part about this kind of dancing is that your bodies have to really become one in order to move as one. So, in other words, I had to learn how to be a real good partner in order to lead correctly."

And here's what Jennifer Grey had to say about partnering:

"Dirty Dancing is really fun, sexy, exciting dancing. But you really don't want to do it with somebody you don't like, you know–it *is* sexy like that. If you put on the right song, have the right dance partner–it can be very fun….Dancing with a man who leads well is essential.

"If this movie will bring back partner dancing, I'd be very happy. It's so romantic!"

Baby and Johnny's Mambo together in
perfect harmony.

## MAMBO

When Patrick Swayze was asked to describe the Mambo, he said, ''The Mambo is like a heartbeat, starting on the second beat. The feeling in Mambo is that it has to feel like butter, loose but with tension.''

Remember the first time you see a Mambo in *Dirty Dancing?* Johnny and Penny come out and dazzle the room. Their moves were based, of course, on years of training and partnering together. The best way for you to learn the Mambo is to watch what all the other dancers in the room were doing. Most of them were practicing the basic Mambo steps which are virtually the same as the Rumba, an African dance. The Mambo is based on Element 3, the Rocking Step. Again, each step is done on a beat.

*Man*
1. Move Left Foot to side.
2. Right and Left close together.
3. Left forward.
4. Right to the side.
5. Left and Right close together.
6. Move Right Foot backward.

*Woman*
1. Move Right Foot to side.
2. Left and Right close together.
3. Right backward.
4. Left to side.
5. Right and Left close together.
6. Move Left Foot forward.

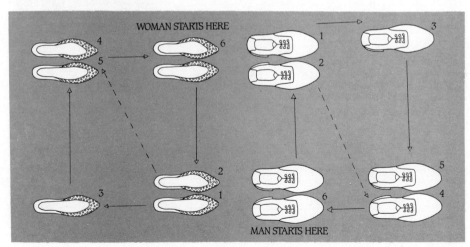

WOMAN STARTS HERE

MAN STARTS HERE

**Keep your weight on the balls of your feet when doing Latin dances.**

*Man*

1. Complete one Mambo Box.
2. Raise Left Arm to signal a turn.
3. Begin another Box.
4. Turn partner using pressure from Right Hand.
5. Finish turn with one more Box.

*Woman*

1. Finish first Box.
2. Point Right Foot to angle, stepping into turn.
3. Curve Left Foot forward to mid-circle, turning under partner's arm.

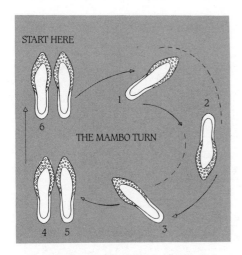

START HERE

THE MAMBO TURN

6

1

2

4  5

3

4. Curve Right Foot forward to complete with turn.
5. Close Right and Left to face partner.

Stay on the ball of your foot at all times– stepping down on your heel looks sloppy and takes away from your timing; you will be moving quite fast to Mambo music and can't loose your position by putting your heel down. Also remember to keep your wrists relaxed.

Finally, add hip motion to the basic steps. Now you can add all the breaks you want.

## CHA-CHA

The Cha-cha is a combination of the Rocking Step, Element 3, and the triple step, which is easy to remember if you say 1-2, cha–cha–cha. So the Cha-cha rhythm is 1-2, 1-2-3. Rocking Step, cha–cha–cha.

**An unusual way to learn how to Cha-cha!**

## Man

1. Move Left forward.*
2. Right stays in place.
3. Left steps backward.
4. Right moves backward.
5. Left moves backward.
6. Right foot backward on ball of foot.
7. Left stays in place.
8. Right forward.
9. Left forward.
10. Right forward.

## Woman

1. Move Right backward on ball of foot.
2. Left stays in place.
3. Right steps forward.
4. Left moves forward.
5. Right forward.
6. Left forward.
7. Right stays in place.
8. Left backward.
9. Right backward.
10. Left backward.

*Always use small steps to move backward and forward.

Now add your hip motion!

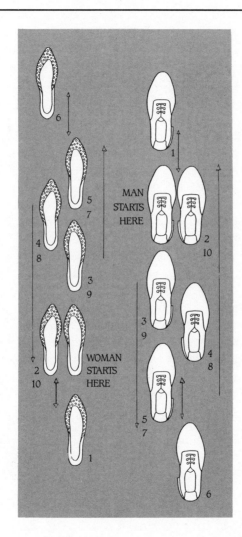

## PRACTICING DIRTY DANCING

Dirty Dancing is hot. Dirty Dancing is done with a partner. Tight. Close. Together.

The most important element in Dirty Dancing will be your hips. These hips have to learn how to move'n'groove.

The absolute best way to learn how to Dirty Dance is to watch the movie. And you really need to have it on video-cassette so you can watch it in slow-motion, and put the pause button on while you practice the steps.

Each time you watch the film, pick out one specific couple to look at, and mimic their moves. Practice by yourself at first, only doing what you can, and then moving on to different steps done by a different couple. It's very important to practice the basic moves by yourself, in front of a full-length mirror, before getting a partner.

Never, ever attempt to do back bends or lifts without proper training, or your Dirty Dancing days will be over before they've even begun! All the Dirty Dancers in the movie were trained professionals with years of experience. They know how to keep their bodies limber and very specific muscles, used for dancing and more gymnastic moves, toned and strong. The only person who can show you how to do more advanced moves is a professional dance teacher.

### HIP CIRCLES
1. Start with feet apart. Arms down, relaxed, at your sides (*not* at waist level as for Latin dances), but out of the way of your Hip Circle.
2. Bend knees slightly.
3. Push hips forward.
4. Move your hips around in a circle. Forward–right–back–left–forward. Now reverse direction: Forward–left–back–right–forward.

Some kind of Cha-cha!

## DIRTY DANCING TOGETHER

Now, get your partner. Hold each other close. Your arms should be resting on your partner's shoulders, or waist, or even on the neck. This is fairly informal partnering so you don't need to hold the more rigid partner position of Latin dancing.

Hip circles.

Remember, though, even in Dirty Dancing the man leads. Because you are holding each other unusually close, it's very easy to sense a change in your partner's movements. This is what makes Dirty Dancing look so sexy and fluid when it's done properly.

## DO'S AND DON'TS

*DO* watch as many old dance films as you can. Study the dances, their turns, the way the dancers hold themselves. You can incorporate any moves from them into your own routines.

*DO* buy a full-length mirror (if you haven't already got one) so you can practice effectively.

*DO* find a partner who's as motivated as you are to get down and boogie. (There's nothing wrong with practicing with a person of the same sex if there's no one around of the opposite sex!)

*DO* practice listening for the beat in songs and improving your rhythm.

*DO* wear proper shoes.

*DO* stop when you feel tired. Otherwise you'll start making mistakes and only get flustered.

*DO* have a great sense of humor. If you can't laugh at your mistakes and enjoy yourself, you'll miss all the fun.

*DO* practice as much as you can. And get out there and dance!

*DON'T* get frustrated or discouraged. Dancing is not as easy as it looks! But the more you practice the easier it becomes–really! Everyone starts out with two left feet and hips with a life of their own.

*DO NOT* attempt any moves you're not sure of–like deep back bends, deep-knee bends, or, most especially, lifts. You and your partner can get seriously injured without proper training.

*DON'T* give up on your partner if he or she isn't as fast a learner as you are. Every dancer picks up skill, coordination, and movements at his or her own speed and ability.

*DON'T* forget to drink lots of water while you practice.

*DON'T* stop exercising or working out if you do so already. The better shape you're in, the more quickly you can progress to more complicated moves.

*DON'T* compare yourself to other dancers. Stop thinking how much better they are (they're probably only different, anyway). You're dancing for *you*.

The man leads with his knee, not his hands. The woman is turned slightly away from him, and instead of facing him straight, she is positioned against the man's right leg.

Bend your knees.
Move your hips–together–from side to side.
Do Hip Circles.
To the right. To the left. Backward. Forward.

Didn't think dancing could be so much fun, did you?

## HIP CIRCLE VARIATION

Woman stands straight.
Man does a Hip Circle.
Now the woman does a Hip Circle.
You are mirror images of each other.
You can do this backward and forward, or from side to side.
Let the man lead.

## KNEE BEND SPECIAL

The woman does Hip Circles.
The Man does deep-knee bends while circling with his hips at the same time. (This is NOT easy. If you're not quite so limber, the man can get down on his knees, on the floor, and do Hip Circles from this position while the woman remains standing. It can look just as effective this way.)
Now try it with the man doing standing Hip Circles and the woman going down to the floor.

## DIRTY DANCE GRAND CIRCLE

Man does the basic Hip Circles.
The woman walks around him in a circle, moving her hips all the while.
Reverse positions.

## LEG LICKS

The woman does the basic Hip Circles.
The man goes down, in a spiral–keeping to the beat of the Hip Circle–all the way down the woman's leg to the floor, and slowly travels back up her leg.
Now, repeat it with the woman going down the man's leg.
Remember to remain in place for this.
You can both go down together, as well.
Keep your knees bent at all times!

The Jerk.

## SWINGSET

Knees bent. Woman kicks to right with her Right Leg. Man kicks to left with his Left Leg.

Bring feet together.

Repeat the kicks with opposite leg: Woman kicks with Left Leg; man kicks with Right.

You can step-kick from side to side, or back and forth. The swinging motion makes you look like a swingset!

## THE JERK

Partners face each other, but hands free.

Do the jerk, in opposite directions.

To do the jerk, you use your shoulders and arms. Put your Right Arm straight up in the air. Now bend it 90 degrees at the elbow. Your forearm should be at forehead height. The fingers of your Right Hand point to the left, and they should be positioned just over your left shoulder.

Place Left Arm in opposite direction– fingers pointing to the right, at the Right Shoulder–down at about chin level.

Make arms switch places with each
other–right on top, left on top–by
jerking your chest backward and
forward.

You can also move arms–from below the
elbow–back and forth, without keeping them at a 90-degree angle in front
of the body.

## SPANISH DRAG

In this very popular move, the man sways
the woman from side to side. It's the first
move Baby and Johnny do when she comes
to his room the night they did the Mambo
Magic number together. The Spanish Drag is
actually based on a dance move that origi-
nated with the Tango.

The man pulls the woman very close. He
wraps his Right Arm around her lower
back and gently but firmly sways her
back and forth, or from side to side.

The woman must keep her knees flexed
and her neck relaxed. You must trust
your partner! The man does nearly all
of the work in this move.

He can move the woman slowly, or quick-
quick-slow.

You should look like two reeds swaying in
the wind.

The Spanish Drag—swaying from side to
side while Dirty Dancing.

The man must remember to keep a slight counter-pull in his weight, or the woman will topple backward. Keep your hand, fingers splayed, firmly on her mid-back.

## BACK AND FORTH

Holding each other tight, the man bends his back slightly. Keep the neck relaxed.

The woman follows him, arching her back forward.

Repeat the motion, the woman going backward and the man following her forward.

You can do this move all the way around in a slow circle if you like.

If you don't want to do any back bending, just follow each other in slow circles–as the man goes back, the woman goes forward, or vice versa.

## SHOULDER TO SHOULDER

Woman makes a circle with her shoulder; the man is her mirror image.

As she moves her Right Shoulder in a circle forward, he moves his Left Shoulder in a circle backward.

Repeat with the other shoulder. Woman moves her Left Shoulder in a circle forward; the man moves his Right Shoulder backward.

Now repeat with the woman moving back, then forward.

Shoulder circles are not an up-and-down motion, but one that goes back and forth. The man and woman are not actually touching their shoulders when they do this properly.

The best way to practice getting a fluid motion from your shoulders is to repeat the motion over and over again in front of a full-length mirror or even up against a wall. Do a shoulder circle so the front of the circle actually touches–very lightly–the wall or mirror.

Keep practicing–as with the Hip Circles–until the motion is very easy for you to do.

## DOUBLE UP HIP-TO-HIP

Instead of simply facing each other, the man bends his Right Leg slightly and the woman straddles it.

He puts his Right arm around her waist, leaving his Left Arm free. Her Right Arm is free, and her Left Arm is around his waist.

Woman bends back slightly at the waist.

Now do your Hip Circles together.

Repeat by shifting over to the man's Left Leg.

## BACK TO FRONT

You can do almost any of the Dirty Dance moves in a different position:

Instead of the woman facing the man, she turns his back on him. His hands can rest lightly on her waist, or her neck, or on her upper thighs.

Now do your Hip Circles together. Try and move down all the way to the floor if you can.

If the man is strong, he can do partial back bends–or, if he likes, he can simply sway back and forth, and the woman follows his lead and leans back into his weight.

Shoulder-to-Shoulder.

## SOME TIPS FROM A PRO

"Dirty Dancing is like sex on legs!" jokes professional dancer Susie Thomas. She has danced with the Sadler's Wells Royal Ballet in England and the National Ballet of Portugal, as well as in the casts of the musicals *Chess* and *Carrie*. "It's very sensual, very much a partner thing, and very natural. You can either wiggle or not! It's actually just about getting completely wild.

"Because I've been classically trained, like Patrick Swayze, people are always asking me how to do Dirty Dancing. But it's not really choreography, like ballroom dancing. It's just you. That's what can be so wonderful about it. When I Dirty Dance, I'm doing it for me—it's just me and the music. I'm not 'on'; I'm not working. It should be fun. It's not about you caring what you look like or wondering what everybody else on the dance floor thinks of you or worrying if you've got the steps right. You've just got to let go, and do what the music tells you."

# AFTERWORD

The movie musical is about as American as apple pie, but there have been relatively few recent films in which dancing is so integral to the plot, each sequence seemlessly propelling the action forward...without interrupting it. When successful, like the marvelous scene when Baby, in Johnny's cabin, says to him, ''Dance with me,'' and it becomes their dance of love, a wonderful dance sequence can be far more eloquent and charged with emotion than any dramatic confrontation.

*Saturday Night Fever*, of course, did for disco what *Dirty Dancing* did for Dirty Dancing. A few years later its star, John Travolta, briefly caused a flurry of interest in the Texas two-step in *Urban Cowboy*. (Incidentally, that movie was choreographed by none other than Patrick's mother, Patsy Swayze.) Both *Footloose* and *Flashdance* (which also featured Cynthia Rhodes) used dance doubles in place of their stars in the extended dance sequences, and this often strained credulity and led to camouflaged editing. Everything in *Dirty Dancing* was danced by its stars.

There will undoubtedly be many more films to come–like *Salsa* and *Shag*–that attempt to integrate dancing into the plot. But none of them will ever make us feel like dancing like *Dirty Dancing* did.

I had the time of my life…and I owe it all to you.

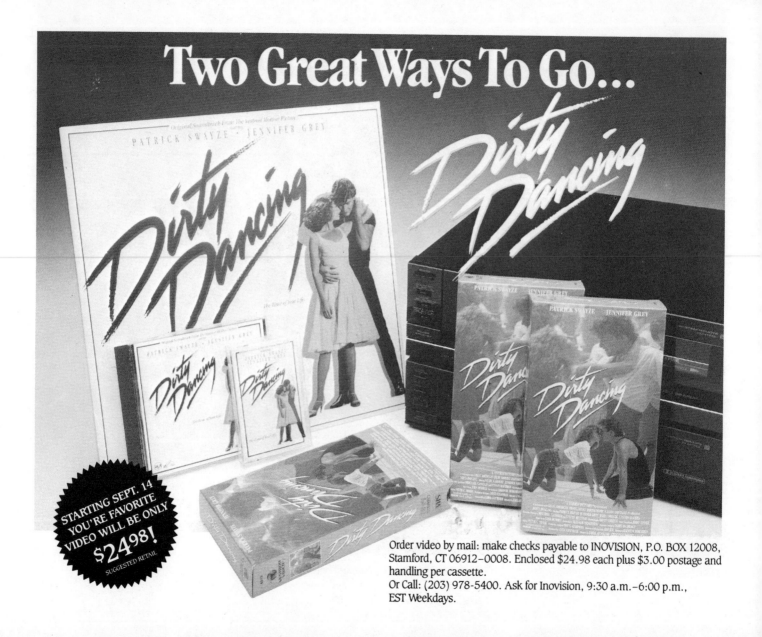